Contents

Meet → AVA

Hello! My name is Ava. I'm seven years old and I am Deaf. Deaf people's ears work differently to hearing people's. There are about nine million Deaf people in the UK, but each one is different – some of them can't hear anything, while others can hear some sounds.

I live in London with my mum and dad who are also Deaf. Deaf people often write the word Deaf with a capital D because they are proud to be Deaf. Our deafness makes us unique, and means we get to be part of a wonderful community. Deaf people can achieve amazing things!

DEAF ☆ ACHIEVER ...

In July 2016, 48-year-old Andrew Rees became the first Deaf person to swim the English Channel solo.

BRITISH SIGN LANGUAGE

I use British Sign Language, a language that uses the hands, body and face instead of the voice. It has signs for each letter of the alphabet, as well as for all the words and phrases that people use every day.

More than 150,000 Deaf people use British Sign Language (BSL) as their main language. Thousands of hearing people also use BSL, usually if they have friends or family who are Deaf — my grandparents, uncle and auntie are hearing, but use BSL with me and my parents.

This is my grandmother. I call her Poppy!

There's lots of BSL to learn at the back of the book.

BSL gives you communication superpowers. You can talk easily underwater, through windows, or in a very noisy room – which is useful for parties! You can also talk with your mouth full, and in quiet places like the cinema or the library without bothering anyone. It's great!

People who use BSL have a special sign name so you don't have to spell out each letter of their name every time. Your sign name is given to you by a Deaf person – my dad gave me mine – and is usually based on a feature or habit you have. When I was a baby, I grabbed my face at the same time as sucking my thumb. It's stuck with me ever since!

This is my sign name.

ALL SIGN LANGUAGES ARE → UNIQUE

Do you have a teacher, neighbour or friend who speaks differently to you because they grew up somewhere else? The same thing happens in British Sign Language – there are many 'accents'.

The signs used in Scotland, Wales, England and Northern Ireland are all a bit different from each other, and each city or region often has its own accent too. For example, people in Manchester sign their numbers differently to people in London. All these variations mean we've ended up with about 40 different signs for 'purple' used around Britain!

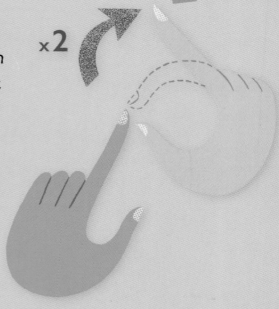

This is one of the signs for purple.

x2

This is the hand sign for the letter 'B' in BSL ...

... and this is the sign for 'B' in ASL!

British Sign Language is not international – other countries have their own sign language. Australian Sign Language and British Sign Language are similar in some ways, since they both use two hands for the alphabet. However, American Sign Language (ASL) only uses one hand, so it's quite different.

There are International Signs that are used when Deaf people from more than one country come together. It's amazing, because you can travel anywhere in the world and communicate with

This is me in Thailand when I was little!

Deaf people wherever you are! Deaf people are usually very friendly and love to show you their homes and culture.

My MUM and DAD

My parents are called Lilli and Nick. They're both Deaf, like me.

My mum has just got a degree in psychology, which is a subject that studies the mind. She wants to become a psychology doctor one day so that she can help people's minds.

My mum is also an in-vision presenter. This is when someone signs in the corner of TV programmes or on handheld screens at museums – they're interpreting spoken English into BSL. My mum also used to present television programmes made especially for Deaf and hard-of-hearing people.

My dad is a designer. His office is in a busy part of London with very tall buildings – his job looks easy to me, but he disagrees!

My dad once captained Great Britain to a football gold medal in the Deaflympics in Australia. The Deaflympics are sporting events for top Deaf athletes around the world. They happen every four years, just like the Olympics.

DEAF ★ ACHIEVER ...

Terence Parkin is a South African swimmer who has won 34 Deaflympics medals in swimming and cycling – and he won a silver medal at the 2000 Sydney Summer Olympics in the 200 m breaststroke.

Life at HOME

Since my mum, my dad and I are all Deaf, our home might be a little bit different from yours.

We have flashing lights in each room – if someone presses the doorbell, a light in each room flashes on and off and the house becomes a disco! If the smoke alarm goes off, the lights also flash to let us know – they're very bright so we wake up if we're asleep.

My dad has a vibrating alarm clock under his pillow. The vibrations are so strong that it's impossible to sleep through. Then he wakes up me and my mum.

This light flashes brightly when the doorbell is rung.

If my parents want to make a voice call, they use a text service on their mobile phones. They talk by typing words to a 'relay assistant', who speaks my parents' words to the hearing person they are calling. The relay assistant then types the hearing person's spoken reply back to my mum or dad for them to read on their mobile phones.

When we watch TV, we always have the subtitles turned on so we know what is being said. Subtitles display the words people on TV are saying near the bottom of the screen.

DEAF ★ ACHIEVER ...

Marlee Matlin is the first Deaf person to have won an Academy Award for acting. She won the Best Actress Oscar in 1986 for a film called *Children of a Lesser God*, in which she used American Sign Language.

At my → SCHOOL

I'm the only Deaf child at my primary school – at first, I didn't notice that I was different from the other students, but as I've got older, I've learned that I'm unique.

Because I don't use or hear speech, I have interpreters who sign to me during lessons. They sign to me what my teachers and classmates are saying, and then tell them what I'm signing back.

This is Marcel. He's great!

My friends at school can all sign, but Emily and Emmy are best of all. They learned sign language from me and a BSL teacher. During lunchtimes and at after-school language clubs, the teacher tells stories in BSL and shows my friends how to sign.

My friends love talking to me in BSL and like to learn new signs. Emily's favourite BSL sign is 'butterfly'. My friends are proud that they now know another language!

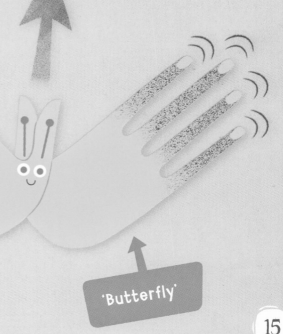

'Butterfly'

My Deaf → FRIENDS

I love having Deaf friends as well as hearing friends. We can sign to each other very quickly and we laugh about the same things! I don't see my Deaf friends as often as I'd like, though – some live a long way away. That's because there are far fewer Deaf kids than hearing kids around the UK.

I see some of my Deaf friends at a local monthly Deaf club and sometimes they come round to my house to play beforehand.

I go to events organised by a group called Deaf Parents Deaf
Children, where I meet and sign with lots of other Deaf kids
who have Deaf parents like I do. They are my favourite
weekends of the year – I get to see all my Deaf friends at
the same time and sign non-stop!

I sometimes meet my Deaf friends in London, at the Science
Museum's monthly BSL-led workshops, or at the National
Portrait Gallery's BSL-interpreted illustration workshops.

MY many! HOBBIES

I have lots of hobbies. Some of my favourites are gymnastics, football, drawing, playing board games, Irish dancing and walking dogs.

Cool moves!

I have gymnastics training every Thursday and I love it. I'm very lucky because I have trainee BSL interpreters there. I have a competition coming up so I've been practising my routine at home – I rearrange the living room with cushions so it's my own gymnasium!

I love to dance. That might sound odd, but if the music is loud I can feel and follow the rhythm through my feet. I went to a festival last week and I danced with everyone in front of the live bands. I liked bhangra dancing the most!

My family looks after other people's dogs for fun. I love playing with dogs and giving them a sign name. My favourite dog is Twiglet. Her sign name means 'ball', because she likes playing fetch so much.

DEAF ☆ ACHIEVER

Ashley Fiolek is a professional motocross racer. She won the Women's Motocross Championship in 2008, 2009, 2011 and 2012!

Out and → ABOUT

My family loves to go out and about – we go to museums, the theatre and the park.

When I'm out and about and someone doesn't know I'm deaf, I point to my ear and lip-speak, "I am deaf". I feel more shy with hearing people who can't sign, but I like it when they make an effort. We went to California once and lots of hearing people knew the ASL alphabet – it made me feel very happy.

If someone doesn't know any BSL, I can use simple hand gestures to get across what I mean – or I can write things down on a piece of paper or type messages on a phone. Sometimes I can lip-read what is being said to me.

I wanted to know how much this little lantern was, so I wrote a message to the shopkeeper.

Lip-reading is when you work out what someone is saying by watching the way their mouth moves when they speak. It's easier for me if I have an idea of what the person will be talking about, if they are looking straight at me and if they are talking at a nice relaxed pace with gestures.

MY hearing → AIDS

I have hearing aids for both my ears. Hearing aids help by making sounds louder, but they work differently for each Deaf person. For some, hearing aids can make them hear all kinds of sounds, including speech.

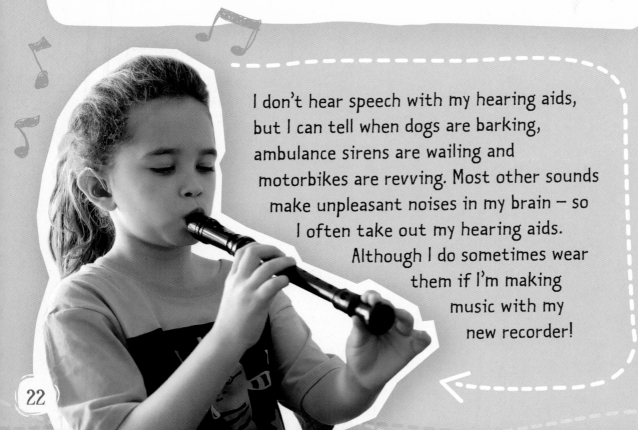

I don't hear speech with my hearing aids, but I can tell when dogs are barking, ambulance sirens are wailing and motorbikes are revving. Most other sounds make unpleasant noises in my brain – so I often take out my hearing aids. Although I do sometimes wear them if I'm making music with my new recorder!

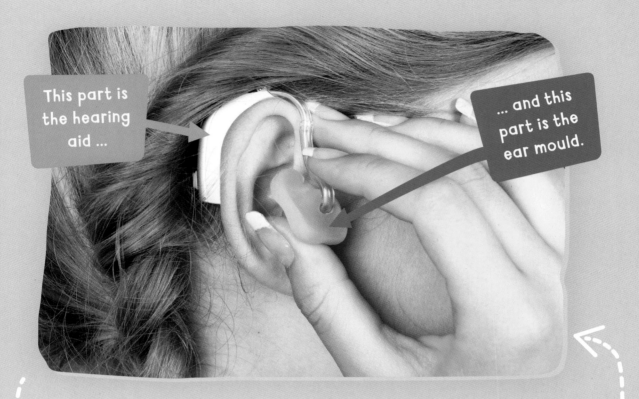

This part is the hearing aid ...

... and this part is the ear mould.

Hearing aids have to be fitted by an audiologist, which is someone who looks after people's ears and hearing. When I visit my audiologist, she gives me a style menu that has lots of colours to choose from. My hearing aids are red, because that's one of my favourite colours. My latest ear moulds are pink with purple swirls and silver glitter.

I have to have new ear moulds fitted every four months because my ears are always growing — if the moulds become too small for my ears, the hearing aids start to whistle and are very annoying for other people!

Cochlear → IMPLANTS

Not all Deaf people can hear speech using hearing aids. Sometimes, a cochlear implant might be tried. Cochlear (say 'cock-lee-are') implants have two parts: one part is worn like a hearing aid, and receives and sends sounds, while the second part sends these sounds to the brain. The second part is implanted surgically, behind the ear.

Cochlear implants can sometimes help people who are completely Deaf to hear more than they could with hearing aids. The sounds aren't exactly what a hearing person would hear — speech sounds a bit like a robot talking — but the Deaf person is hearing things they otherwise would not be able to. Some of my Deaf friends have cochlear implants — but listening can be quite hard work for them, so they love using BSL too.

Not all Deaf people can have a cochlear implant, and they don't always work. Besides, some Deaf people, like me and my family, like being Deaf just the way we are!

DEAF ★ ACHIEVER ...

Andrew Foster was the first black person to graduate from Gallaudet University, the only Deaf university in the world. He opened 32 Deaf schools in 13 African countries.

VOCALISING

Speaking with your voice is called 'vocalising', and many Deaf people don't learn to do it when they're babies like hearing people do. Since we don't hear ourselves speak, it's pretty hard for us to tell if we're making the right sounds.

This is my friend Ruth at speech therapy.

Sometimes a Deaf person chooses not to use their voice at all — they mouth words so that a hearing person can lip-read what they're saying. Other Deaf people like to use their voices with hearing people.

I practise vocalising just in case I need to use my voice with people who can't sign. I have speech therapy at school once a week. These sessions teach me to make sounds, practise lip movements and read lips. Still, I don't like vocalising too much because it can make my throat hurt, and I need to remember where my tongue has to go to make each word. For me, signing is the best way to communicate.

My FUTURE

Deaf people can do anything – there are Deaf doctors, scientists, sports stars, chefs, lawyers, builders and teachers! It's hard for me to decide what I want to do when I grow up because there are so many options!

At the moment I'm choosing between being a vet and a famous actress.

My friend Rosa wants to be a zookeeper, Alex wants to be an actor and film director, and Saskia wants to be an artist who draws Japanese cartoons!

Rosa

Alex

DEAF ★ ACHIEVER ...

John Denerley is a wildlife conservationist. He runs the Galloway Wildlife Conservation Park in Scotland, where he works to protect endangered animals.

Being a good HEARING FRIEND

I love my hearing friends. Here are my top tips for communicating with Deaf people so you can make a Deaf friend!

TOP TIPS when talking to a Deaf person

⭐ To get their attention, you can wave or tap their shoulder

⭐ Face them so that you can be lip-read more easily

⭐ Try to make your mouth shapes as clear as possible

⭐ Don't put your hands in front of your face

⭐ Make sure it's clear what the topic of conversation is – don't switch to a new one without warning

⭐ Speak to one person at a time, and try not to interrupt

⭐ Check if they understand – if not, try a different way of communicating, such as using pen and paper

⭐ Never give up

British Sign Language

⭐ Facial expressions are great! If you use a smiley face while telling a happy story and an angry face while telling a bad story, it really helps. If you're asking a question, raise your eyebrows

⭐ If you don't know a certain word in BSL, use finger-spelling instead (see the next page). Even just the first letter of each word can really help

⭐ Don't be afraid to make mistakes

⭐ Try not to be shy

Turn the page to discover lots of BSL words and phrases. If you need help, visit our YouTube channel to see videos of the signs. Find the web address on page 47.

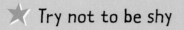

THE BSL ALPHABET

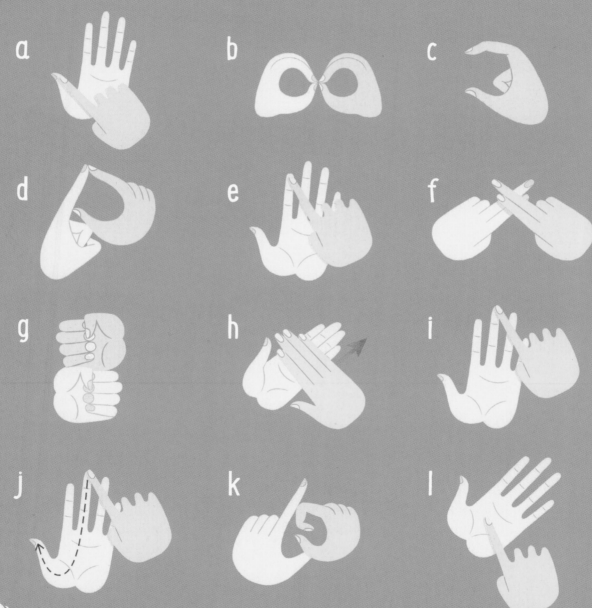

a b c
d e f
g h i
j k l

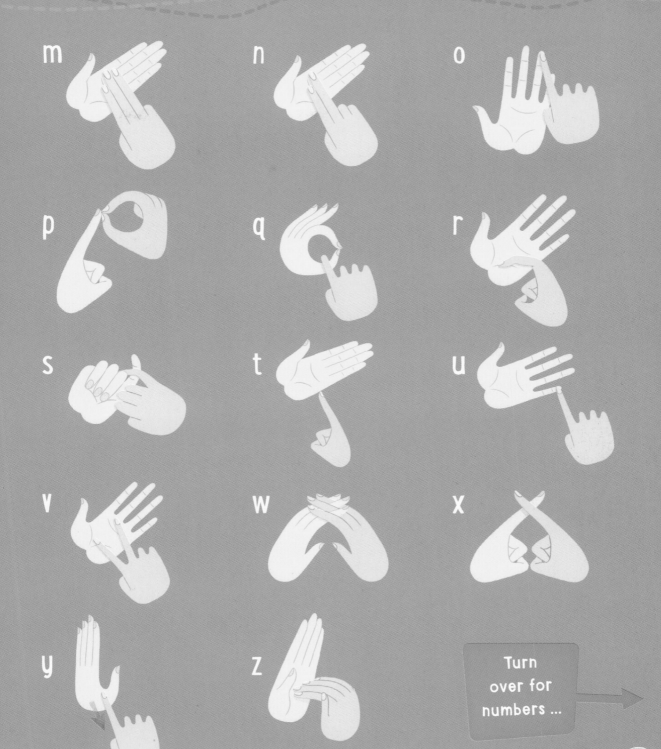

Turn over for numbers ...

BSL → NUMBERS

0

1

2

3

4

5

6

7

8

9

10

11

12

13

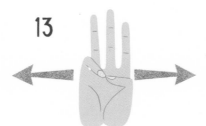

14

15

16

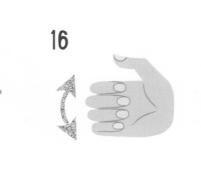

17

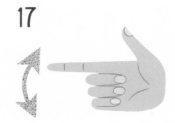

18

19

20

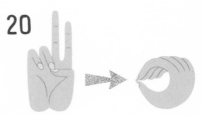

BSL → QUESTIONS

Rather than spelling out everything using the alphabet, BSL has signs for all sorts of different questions. BSL grammar is different to English grammar. The signs below feature Sign Supported English, which can be easier for first-time BSL learners.

What's your name?

How old are you?

What would you like to eat?

What's your favourite colour?

Where do you live?

BSL → IMPORTANT WORDS

If you want to learn BSL, these helpful linking and question words will give you a great head start.

Want

Don't want

And

Can

Can't

But

BSL → TOPICS

Days of the week

Monday

x2

Tuesday

x2

Wednesday

x2

Thursday

1 2 3

Friday

Saturday

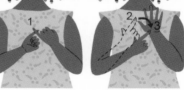
1 2 3

Sunday

x2

Food

Vegetables

Fruit

Chocolate

x2

Red   Yellow   Blue

Colours

Cat   Dog   Bird

Animals

Happy   Nervous   Sad

Feelings

BSL → IN THE PLAYGROUND

Here are some of my favourite words to use during breaks at school!

Best friend

Do you want to play?

Football

Tag

Hide and seek

Run

Playground

43

BSL → OUT AND ABOUT

I've given you lots of BSL words and phrases, but here's a useful tip: if you want to use a word you don't know the sign for, mouth it while making the sign for the letter it starts with. It'll be a big help!

Beach

Countryside

Town

Farm

Swimming pool

Holiday

England

Scotland

Great Britain

Northern Ireland

Wales

School

Home

Park

Tree house

Words to remember

audiologist Someone who does hearing tests. They also make ear moulds and fit hearing aids.

bhangra A type of popular music that mixes folk music from Punjab, India with dance music from America and Europe.

British Sign Language (BSL) A language that uses movement of the hands, body, face and head.
It is the first or preferred language for many Deaf people in the UK.

cochlear implant (CI) A surgically implanted electronic device that can sometimes provide a sense of sound to a person who is profoundly Deaf or severely hard of hearing in both ears.

communication The act of transferring information from one person to another.

community A group of people who share the same interests.

conservationist Someone who works to protect and preserve wildlife and the environment.

degree An important certificate given to someone when they complete their studies at a university or college.

ear mould A piece of plastic or other material moulded to fit in the ear, which delivers the sound from a hearing aid.

gestures A movement of a part of the body, especially a hand or the head, to express an idea.

hearing aid A small electronic device that you wear in or behind the ear. It makes some sounds louder so that a Deaf person can hear things.

interpreter Someone who interprets, or translates, one language into another language.

in-vision presenter Someone who appears in the corner of a screen translating spoken words or written English into sign language.

Irish dancing Traditional folk dances from Ireland.

lip-reading A way of understanding spoken words, by studying the movements of the speaker's lips without hearing the sounds.

motocross Cross-country racing on motorcycles.

psychology The scientific study of the human mind and how it works.

relay assistant A phone operator who helps people who are Deaf or hard of hearing to make calls to a hearing person using a keyboard.

Sign Supported English (SSE) A language that borrows signs from British Sign Language (BSL) and follows English grammatical structure. It is used to support spoken English.

speech therapy Sessions that aim to develop vocalising and lip-reading skills.

subtitles Words displayed at the bottom of a cinema or TV to show what is being said.

workshop A meeting where people talk about or do activities about a particular topic.

vibrations Tiny back-and-forth movements.

vocalising Using a voice to create sounds.

ℹ️ further information

⭐ **Proud to be Deaf**

Visit our YouTube channel to see videos of all the signs in the BSL section of this book.

www.youtube.com/channel/UCFjBdGrdLKbi17qpqgt7tXA

⭐ **National Deaf Children's Society**

The National Deaf Children's Society (NDCS) is the UK's leading charity dedicated to creating a world without barriers for Deaf children and young people.

www.ndcs.org.uk

⭐ **British Deaf Association**

The British Deaf Association (BDA) is a Deaf-led UK charity that stands for Deaf equality, access and freedom of choice.

https://bda.org.uk/

⭐ **Deaf Parents Deaf Children**

Deaf Parents Deaf Children (DPDC) is a group for Deaf parents with Deaf children. It aims to show a positive view of deafness, to demonstrate what Deaf people can achieve and to give Deaf parents an equal voice in what happens to their Deaf children.

http://deafparentsdeafchildren.co.uk/

INDEX

THANK YOU

To Tomlinsons, Dulwich, Flashing Lights Media and Brixton Recreation Centre for providing photography locations featured in the book.

To Toby Burton, Emma Burton, Justine Durno, Matt Beese, Suzi Beese, Christine Beese, Mike Beese, Paddy Ladd, Dani Sive, Patrick Rosenburg, Jen Dodds, Marcel Hirshman, Polly Burton, Ag Katz Barlow and Noelia Felgueira Gomez for their support in writing this book. And a special thanks to Hugh Mulloy for everything he contributed.

A.B., L.B. and N.B.